AHOY MCCOY'S PIRATE COOKBOOK

A CULINARY ADVENTURE AROUND THE WORLD

BY CHERRIE AND DENNIS MCCOY

Fulton Books, Inc.
Meadville, PA

Published by Fulton Books 2021

A hearty thanks goes to
Muriel Lee Coolidge Kompolt Szuszitzky
who always said we should write a cookbook!

Thanks to all the Pirate Artists who contributed to this cookbook

ISBN 978-1-64952-815-5 (hardcover)
ISBN 978-1-64952-814-8 (digital)

Printed in the United States of America

I, CAPTAIN DENNY, WOULD LIKE TO THANK THE SHIP'S FAITHFUL COOK, ONE-EYED WILLY, ALONG WITH HIS WACKY SIDEKICK, TOUCAN SALLY, FOR THEIR ENTHUSIASTIC COMMITMENT TO FANTASTIC FOOD AND FABULOUS PIRATE FUN.

THIS PIRATE COOKBOOK IS DEDICATED TO THE PRINCESS OF PURPLE, MY FIRST MATE, LOVING SOUS CHEF, AND BEAUTIFUL WIFE, CHERRIE.

AHOY MCCOY'S PIRATE COOKBOOK

A CULINARY ADVENTURE AROUND THE WORLD

Avast, ye, and welcome aboard me ship o' delicious treasures—the *AHOY MCCOY!* I am Denny, the *AHOY MCCOY*'s captain; and along with me first mate, the purple pirate. We invite you to travel around the world on the open seas to find a treasure trove of mouthwatering meals with tempting exotic flavors.

At each enchanting port on our exciting culinary adventure, we will create tantalizing dishes that are inspired by some of our favorite foods of each region. This pirate ship travel guide will help *YOU* to make these special recipes right in *YOUR* very own galley!

YOU MAY WONDER WHY MY SHIP'S NAME IS *AHOY MCCOY*. WELL, I AM AN IRISH PIRATE PLUNDERING ALL OVER THE WORLD AS ANY OTHER PIRATE WOULD!

THE NAME OF THE SHIP'S COOK IS ONE-EYED WILLY, A CRUSTY OLD SEA DOG WITH ONE EYE, A PEG LEG, AND A BAD SENSE OF HUMOR. NO COMPLAINTS HERE BECAUSE HE IS THE FAITHFUL COOK ABOARD OUR VESSEL AND CAN ALWAYS BE COUNTED ON TO MAKE THE TASTIEST DISHES WE COULD EVER EAT. HE KEEPS THE GALLEY WELL-STOCKED, AND HE WASHES THE DIRTY CROCKERY AS WELL. AGAIN, NO COMPLAINTS HERE!

ANOTHER GALLEY CREWMEMBER IS TOUCAN SALLY. SHE IS QUITE A PARADOX, SPEAKING IN RIDDLES, QUATRAINS, PUNS, TRIPLE ENTENDRE, AND HAIKU. ALTHOUGH SHE CAN BE QUITE CONFUSING, ONE-EYED WILLY PUTS UP WITH IT BECAUSE HE KNOWS THAT HE NEEDS HER HELP IN THE GALLEY FOR THE LONG JOURNEY AROUND THE WORLD ON THE WIDE-OPEN SEAS.

WHEREVER WE GO, ONE-EYED WILLY SCAVENGES FOR LOCAL DELICACIES. HE AND TOUCAN SALLY SEEM TO KNOW PEOPLE EVERYWHERE WE GO. THEY VISIT THESE LOCALS TO PROCURE THE FINEST AND FRESHEST INGREDIENTS IN ALL THE LANDS. WHEN THEY FINALLY RETURN TO THE MIGHTY *AHOY MCCOY* AFTER THEIR TREASURE HUNT FOR EDIBLE BOOTY, THEY WILL PREPARE FANTASTIC SEA-WORTHY MEALS FOR ALL TO ENJOY.

THE FEASTS ARE FIT FOR ROYALTY! PIRATE ROYALTY, THAT IS! BUT BE YE WARNED, ONE-EYED WILLY HAS BEEN KNOWN TO LICK HIS FINGERS TO TASTE THE FOOD WHILE HE COOKS.

JOIN US AS WE SET SAIL ON THE HIGH SEAS IN SEARCH OF THE BEST BOUNTY-O-EATS!

CULINARY CONTENTS

EVERYONE HAS DIFFERENT TASTE BUDS, AND MAY HAVE TO ADD OR REDUCE SALT, PEPPER, CHILI FLAKES, CORNSTARCH OR ALCOHOL. PLEASE OMIT ANY RECIPE INGREDIENT THAT MAY BE TROUBLESOME FOR YOU OR ANYONE IN YOUR CREW.

THE SIDE DISHES SHOWN ARE AN EXAMPLE, SO SERVE WITH YOUR FAVORITES.

CAPITOLA, CALIFORNIA

THE JOURNEY BEGINS ON THE PACIFIC AT OUR HOME PORT OF CAPITOLA ON THE MONTEREY BAY ON THE COAST OF NORTHERN CALIFORNIA. HERE THE TREASURES OF THE SEA COMMAND US TO CREATE OUR LOCAL SPECIALTY, THE BOTTOM FEEDER PATTIES! PICKY PIRATES PROCLAIM THAT THEY LOVE THESE DELICIOUS CRAB CAKES BECAUSE THEY ARE CRUNCHY ON THE OUTSIDE, YET TENDER ON THE INSIDE. THEY ARE UNLIKE ANY OTHER BOTTOM FEEDER PATTIES FOUND IN ANY PORT IN THE KNOWN WORLD, AND THEY WILL MAKE YOU SAY AAARRRRRRGH!

YOU CAN USE FRESH CRAB, OR WHEN THE CRAB TRAPS ARE EMPTY, CANNED CRAB WILL DO. TOUCAN SALLY MAKES SURE WE ARE WELL-STOCKED WITH PROVISIONS IN CANS AS THEY DON'T HAVE TO BE REFRIGERATED, AND THEY KEEP A LONG TIME.

BOTTOM FEEDER PATTIES

INGREDIENTS

12 OUNCES FANCY CRAB MEAT WITH LEG MEAT (DRAIN THE LIQUID)
6 OUNCES PLAIN WHITE CRAB MEAT (DRAIN THE LIQUID)
1/2 CUP BREAD CRUMBS
2 TABLESPOON FINELY CHOPPED YELLOW ONION
2 TABLESPOONS CHOPPED RED BELL PEPPER
1 CLOVE FINELY CHOPPED GARLIC
1/4 CUP OF MAYONNAISE
1 EGG, BEATEN
1 TABLESPOON OF WORCESTERSHIRE SAUCE
1 TABLESPOON OF LEMON JUICE
1/4 TEASPOON OF SALT
1/4 TEASPOON OF WHITE PEPPER
1 TEASPOON OF WHITE WINE
3-4 TABLESPOONS OF COOKING OIL

DIRECTIONS

1. MIX UP ALL THE INGREDIENTS IN A MEDIUM SIZE BOWL.
2. USE YOUR HANDS TO MAKE SIX TO EIGHT SMALL ROUND CAKES AND REFRIGERATE THEM ON A COOKIE SHEET OR LARGE PLATE FOR AT LEAST ONE HOUR.
3. WHEN THE CRAB CAKES ARE CHILLED, WARM A MEDIUM-SIZE FRY PAN ON MEDIUM-HIGH HEAT, AND COAT THE BOTTOM OF THE PAN WITH THREE-FOUR TABLESPOONS OF VEGETABLE OIL.
4. WHEN THE OIL IN THE PAN IS HOT, GENTLY PLACE THE CRAB CAKES INTO THE OIL.
5. COOK THE CRAB CAKES APPROXIMATELY 13 MINUTES OR WHEN THE BOTTOMS ARE DARK GOLDEN BROWN.
6. DELICATELY TURN OVER EACH CRAB CAKE TO COOK THE OTHER SIDE FOR ABOUT 13 MINUTES OR WHEN THE BOTTOMS ARE A DARK GOLDEN BROWN.
7. LINE A COOKIE SHEET WITH PAPER TOWELS AND CAREFULLY TRANSFER CAKES ONTO IT TO ABSORB ANY EXCESS OIL.
8. IF NEEDED, YOU CAN PLACE THE COOKIE SHEET WITH THE CRAB CAKES IN A WARM OVEN UNTIL READY TO SERVE.

THE TASTY CAPER ISLAND TREASURE SAUCE IS WORTH ITS WEIGHT IN GOLD! ONE-EYED WILLY HAS KEPT THIS RECIPE A SECRET FOR MOST OF HIS LIFE, BUT NOW HE SAYS THAT HE IS READY TO SHARE THIS UNREVEALED SECRET WITH YOU. YOU WILL NO LONGER HAVE TO GO DIVING INTO THE DEEP TO LOOK IN DAVY JONES'S LOCKER FOR THIS TREASURE OF A SAUCE.

CAPER ISLAND TREASURE SAUCE

INGREDIENTS

3 TABLESPOONS MAYONNAISE
1 TABLESPOON CATSUP
1 TEASPOON DICED CAPERS
1 TEASPOON LEMON JUICE
1/4 TEASPOON WHITE PEPPER
1/4 TEASPOON DRIED MUSTARD
1 DASH WORCESTERSHIRE SAUCE

DIRECTIONS

MIX ALL INGREDIENTS TOGETHER IN A BOWL; AND ONCE THEY ARE WELL BLENDED, YOU CAN DRIZZLE THE SAUCE OVER THE TOP OF THE CRAB CAKES OR SERVE THE SAUCE ON THE SIDE

BOTTOM FEEDER PATTIES WITH CAPER ISLAND TREASURE SAUCE

SHOWN WITH LANDLUBBER GOLD ROOTS, AVOCADO SALAD, AND JASMINE RICE

MONTEREY, CALIFORNIA

It usually takes many days and nights to travel from one port to another. Fortunately, our next stop is about thirty nautical miles south across the Monterey Bay, which is one of the largest underwater caverns in the world. This bay is special; 'tis a national marine sanctuary, protecting all kinds of mammals and sea creatures. Some of these critters are unique to the area and live in no other place. We'll most likely spot sea otters, seals, dolphins, and whales along the way. Lucky for us (and them), we're not eating exotic and endangered species because there are plenty of good eatin' fish here to pick from. Thar she blows!

The succulent feast that One-Eyed Willy will make for us is the Scrumpi Shrimp Scampi. The recipe has been around since 1920 and has American Italian roots. We put our own garlicky Monterey Bay spin on it to ensure each luscious shrimp melts in your mouth like butter.

WE USE LOTS OF GARLIC, IMPORTED FROM THE NEARBY INLAND SETTLEMENT OF GILROY WITHIN SANTA CLARA COUNTY, WHICH WAS ONCE KNOWN AS THE VALLEY OF HEART'S DELIGHT DUE TO THE THOUSANDS OF ACRES OF BLOOMING FRUIT TREES AND VEGETABLES. LEGEND HAS IT THAT GILROY IS THE GARLIC CAPITAL OF THE WORLD. LEAVE IT TO THAT WILY ONE EYED WILLY AND THAT KRAKEN CALLED TOUCAN SALLY TO LOCATE THE MECCA OF GARLIC RIGHT IN OUR VERY OWN BACKYYAAAAARRRRRRD!

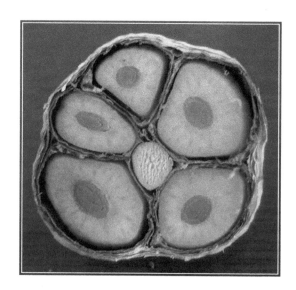

THIS PUNGENT ROOT MAKES THE BODY REEK A FINE ODOR, WHICH IS RATHER HELPFUL IN KEEPING THE FLIES OFF. ONE-EYED WILLY SHOULD EAT MORE GARLIC TO KEEP THE FLIES OUT OF THE KITCHEN!

SCRUMPI SHRIMP SCAMPI

INGREDIENTS

10 PIECES OF 16 TO 20 COUNT JUMBO SHRIMP. REMOVE SHELLS AND DEVEIN
3 TABLESPOONS VEGETABLE OIL
1/2 DICED YELLOW ONION
5 CLOVES DICED GARLIC
1/3 CUP CHOPPED GREEN BELL PEPPER
1/3 CUP CHOPPED RED BELL PEPPER
1/2 TABLESPOON DRIED BASIL
1 TABLESPOON CHOPPED FRESH PARSLEY
1/2 TEASPOON WHITE PEPPER
1 TABLESPOON CAPERS
JUICE OF 1 LEMON
1/2 CUP WHITE WINE
1 TEASPOON CORNSTARCH

DIRECTIONS

1. IN A MEDIUM TO LARGE SIZE SKILLET, HEAT THE OIL ON MEDIUM HEAT.
2. ADD THE ONION, AND COOK ABOUT 5 MINUTES UNTIL TRANSLUCENT.
3. ADD THE GARLIC AND ALL THE BELL PEPPERS AND COOK FOR 5 MINUTES.
4. SPRINKLE IN THE BASIL, PARSLEY, AND WHITE PEPPER AND COOK FOR 3 MINUTES.
5. ADD THE CAPERS, LEMON JUICE, WHITE WINE, AND SHRIMP.
6. COVER WITH A LID; AND TURN THE HEAT DOWN TO LOW AND SIMMER FOR 5 MINUTES.
7. WHEN THE SHRIMP TURNS VERY PINK, TAKE THE LID OFF AND MIX THE CORN-STARCH WITH A LITTLE WATER, ADDING A WEE BIT AT A TIME WHILE CONSTANTLY STIRRING. THICKEN THE SAUCE TO YOUR SATISFACTION.

SCRUMPI SHRIMP SCAMPI

SHOWN WITH BROCCOLI AND RICE PILAF

ACAPULCO, MEXICO

We head much further south on the pacific ocean to acapulco, mexico by using an old trade route. the country of mexico is vast and proudly offers grub from many regions. we know it is a delightful tasting experience that warms our hearts and our mouths because the mexican recipes tend to use a lot of hot peppers! blackbeard said that it is a blessing to have a hand in determining your own fate; so if you prefer, you can opt out as we enjoy the power of peppers.

Our a maze zing green chili chicken casserole uses mild chilies; but if you need more kick, you can add all the hot peppers you crave. toucan sally says it takes two cans of diced green chilies to give this dish its distinctive flavor along with the cheesy goodness.

A MAZE ZING GREEN CHILI
CHICKEN CASSEROLE

INGREDIENTS

2 BONELESS SKINLESS CHICKEN BREASTS
12 CORN TORTILLAS
1 16-OUNCE JAR MEDIUM OR HOT RED SALSA
2 6-OUNCE CANS DICED MILD GREEN CHILIES
1 12-OUNCE CAN CREAM OF CHICKEN SOUP
4 CUPS SHREDDED CHEDDAR CHEESE
1 32-OUNCE CAN GREEN ENCHILADA SAUCE

DIRECTIONS

1. IN FOUR QUARTS OF WATER, BOIL THE CHICKEN UNTIL IT IS NO LONGER PINK INSIDE. LET COOL.
2. SHRED THE CHICKEN USING 2 FORKS. USE 1 FORK TO HOLD THE CHICKEN BREAST IN PLACE ON YOUR CUTTING BOARD, AND USE THE OTHER FORK TO PULL DOWN ON THE MEAT TO SHRED IT INTO APPROXIMATELY 1/2 × 2 INCH PIECES.
3. USING A KNIFE, CUT THE CORN TORTILLAS INTO QUARTERS.
4. COAT AN 8 × 14 INCH CASSEROLE DISH WITH NONSTICK COOKING SPRAY.
5. PUT HALF OF THE RED SALSA EVENLY ON THE BOTTOM OF THE DISH.
6. LAYER HALF OF THE TORTILLA TRIANGLES OVER THE SALSA.
7. PLACE ALL THE CHICKEN OVER THE TORTILLAS AS EVENLY AS POSSIBLE.
8. SPREAD THE GREEN CHILIES EVENLY OVER THE CHICKEN.
9. SMEAR THE CREAM OF CHICKEN SOUP OVER THE GREEN CHILIES.
10. SPRINKLE HALF OF THE SHREDDED CHEESE ALL OVER THE CASSEROLE.
11. LAYER THE REMAINING HALF OF THE TORTILLA TRIANGLES.
12. SPREAD THE REST OF THE JAR OF SALSA OVER THE TRIANGLES.
13. TOP WITH THE REMAINING TWO CUPS OF SHREDDED CHEESE.
14. COVER THE CASSEROLE DISH WITH FOIL AND PUT ON A COOKIE SHEET.
15. PLACE IN OVEN, PREHEATED TO 375 DEGREES.
16. COOK FOR ONE HOUR, MAKING SURE THAT IT BUBBLES FROM THE BOTTOM.
17. WHEN READY, REMOVE THE FOIL; AND COOK AN ADDITIONAL 10 MINUTES.
18. LET COOL 10 MINUTES BEFORE SERVING.
19. IN A SAUCEPAN, HEAT THE GREEN ENCHILADA SAUCE.
20. LADLE THE GREEN ENCHILADA SAUCE UNDER OR OVER EACH SERVING.

ℭANNON BALL MASH IS CALLED GUACAMOLE, AND IT IS MADE OF RIPE AVOCADOS. IT IS EXTREMELY POPULAR IN THESE PARTS AND BACK HOME IN CALIFORNIA. ONE-EYED WILLY AND TOUCAN SALLY KNOW SOMEONE NEARBY WHO HAS AN AVOCADO FARM WITH THE BEST AVOCADOS IN ALL THE LAND.

THIS CREAMY CONCOCTION CAN BE USED AS A TRADITIONAL CONDIMENT FOR A MEAL OR AS A DELIGHTFUL DIP FOR CHIPS. THE SPICY RECIPE WILL KEEP YOU OUT OF THE CROW'S NEST WITH ITS PURPLE ONION, JALAPENO, AND GARLIC MIXTURE. IF YOU DON'T HAVE WHAT IT TAKES TO HANDLE THESE BOLD FLAVORS, SNEAK BELOW DECK AND MAKE SOME WITH LESS.

CANNON BALL MASH

INGREDIENTS

    3 RIPE AVOCADOS
    1 LEMON
    1 DICED TOMATO
    3 CLOVES FINELY DICED GARLIC
    2 TABLESPOONS DICED PURPLE ONION
    1 TABLESPOON DICED JALAPENO PEPPER
    1 TEASPOON CUMIN
    1/4 TEASPOON PEPPER
    1/4 TEASPOON SALT
    CHILI FLAKES TO YOUR TASTE LEVEL

DIRECTIONS

1. REMOVE THE SKIN FROM THE AVOCADOS AND DISCARD THE PIT
2. CUT THE AVOCADO INTO SMALL PIECES; AND WITH A LARGE FORK, SMASH THE AVOCADO SO IT IS CREAMY AND THERE ARE NO LUMPS--UNLESS YOU LIKE LUMPS.
3. SQUEEZE THE LEMON JUICE WITH NO SEEDS OVER THE AVOCADO MUSH.
4. NOW ADD THE REST OF THE INGREDIENTS INTO THE BOWL AND MIX WELL.

WELL, AAAARRRRGHH! WITH A LITTLE LUCK MAYBE ONE-EYED WILLY OR TOUCAN SALLY WILL MAKE SOME FRESH TORTILLA CHIPS FOR THE CANNON BALL MASH.

A MAZE ZING GREEN CHILI CHICKEN

SHOWN WITH SPANISH RICE AND REFRIED BEANS

CERRO AZUL, PERU

Heading further south, we reach Cerro Azul, Peru. The seas have been kind to us; but not in the past, so hang on to your nearest rope or railing because it might be a choppy one. Our next dish is called Peruvian Shipwreck! I'll let you figure out how it got its name.

The beef in this recipe cooks all day, and it makes the whole ship smell wonderful! The time is well worth the wait because the meat is so tender; you don't need any wooden teeth to savor these meaty morsels! It is so good you'll want to make a double batch to ensure there are plenty of leftovers for your hungry crew.

When we are docked in Peru, One-Eyed Willy seems to get into all kinds of trouble when he goes scavenging. For example, he and Toucan Sally will say that they are going on a quest for the finest Peruvian potatoes, and we won't see them for days on end. We'll all have to wait on the ship eating hard tack biscuits!

When they do finally return, their load is more alpaca fiber than food and no potatoes! They will say they were looking for worthy ingredients and somehow simply got lost. They seem to end up either in Machu Picchu or out at Lake Titicaca. Toucan Sally has a new purple scarf, and she boasts that alpaca cloth is five times warmer than sheep's wool. So long it's not itchy, that's what I say! We don't eat alpaca cloth, but we do like to eat good food. The rest of the crew's cooking is awful, so we are extremely happy to have them back.

SHOWN WITH SPANISH RICE AND PINTO BEANS

PERUVIAN SHIPWRECK

INGREDIENTS

1 1/2 POUNDS STEW MEAT OR YOUR FAVORITE BEEF CUT INTO SMALL BITE SIZE
    PIECES. WE USE LONDON BROIL FOR THIS RECIPE, BUT ANY ANIMAL WILL DO.
4 TABLESPOONS COOKING OIL
1 MEDIUM CHOPPED YELLOW ONION
3 CLOVES CHOPPED GARLIC
8 OUNCES TOMATO SAUCE
8 OUNCES DICED MILD GREEN CHILIES
1 CUP RED WINE, PLUS MORE AS WE COOK
3 TABLESPOONS RED WINE VINEGAR
1 TEASPOON OREGANO
2 BAY LEAVES
1/2 TEASPOON SALT
1/4 TEASPOON PEPPER
1 TABLESPOON RED CHILI FLAKES

DIRECTIONS

1. IN A MEDIUM TO LARGE SIZE POT, HEAT THE COOKING OIL ON MEDIUM HEAT.
2. WHEN THE OIL IS HOT, ADD THE MEAT AND COOK UNTIL NO LONGER PINK.
3. ADD THE ONION AND COOK UNTIL THE ONION IS TRANSLUCENT.
4. ADD THE GARLIC AND COOK FOR 5 MINUTES.
5. STIR IN THE REST OF THE INGREDIENTS, AND ONCE IT COMES TO A BOIL, REDUCE THE HEAT TO LOW AND SIMMER FOR 3 HOURS.

AS IT REDUCES, YOU MAY NEED TO ADD MORE WINE. TOUCAN SALLY HAS USED A WHOLE BOTTLE OF WINE, AND THE CREW LOVED IT! THEY ALL SURVIVED, SO YOU CAN FREELY ADD MORE WINE IF YOU FEEL INSPIRED. THE STEW SHOULD BE THICK SO YOU MAY NEED TO COOK IT LONGER IF IT SEEMS TOO SOUPY. THIS MAGNIFICENT MEAT WILL SURELY GET ALL HANDS ON DECK!

PERUVIAN SHIPWRECK

SHOWN WITH SPANISH RICE AND PINTO BEANS

SANTA CRUZ, ARGENTINA

THE *AHOY MCCOY* EMBARKS ON THE BEAUTIFUL BLUE SEAS TO THE ISLAND OF SANTA CRUZ, ARGENTINA. IF WE'RE LUCKY, MOTHER NATURE WILL PROVIDE SMOOTH SAILING; AND WE CAN TAKE THE SHORTCUT USING THE STRAIT OF MAGELLAN, BUT SOMETIMES THE GALE WINDS THAT MAY COME UP THROUGH THAT PASSAGE COULD MAKE IT TOO ROUGH FOR OUR TRUSTY SHIP. IF THAT IS THE CASE, WE'LL HAVE TO CIRCUMNAVIGATE THE LONGER WAY TO GET AROUND THE SOUTHERNMOST TIP OF SOUTH AMERICA BY FOLLOWING THE DRAKE PASSAGE TO THE ATLANTIC. YET THAT ROUTE CAN ALSO HAVE HORRENDOUSLY TREACHEROUS WEATHER. EITHER WAY, THE *AHOY MCCOY* IS AT RISK OF BEING BEATEN UP. SUCH IS THE LIFE OF A PIRATE.

WE CAN ALWAYS RELY ON OUR EXPERIENCED SAILING MASTER, ONE-ARMED LEFTY, TO KNOW THE WEATHER FORECAST AND THE BEST WAY FOR US TO SAFELY SAIL TO MAKE PASSAGE. WELL ALMOST ALWAYS BECAUSE ON MORE THAN ONE OCCASION, WE HAVE BEEN WAY OFF COURSE! WE ONLY HAVE ONE SAILING MASTER, SO WE JUST GO WITH THE FLOW.

ONE-EYED WILLY HAS A FRIEND ON THE ISLAND WHO HAS THE BEST LEMONS IN ALL THE LAND. HE NEEDS THE TANGY LEMONS FOR HIS FAMOUS LAND LUBBER'S LEMON SAUCE THAT THE CREW ADORES.

HE ALSO NEEDS FRESH TILAPIA SO HE CAN MAKE THE TANTALIZING FESTIVAL ON A PLATE THAT WE ALL CRAVE, THE SHIVER ME TIMBERS TILAPIA. I'LL BE ON THE SHIP WITH THE REST OF 'EM, AND WE'LL PUT OUR HOOKS IN THE WATER FOR SOME GREAT TILAPIA; AND WHEN YOU EAT IT, YOU WILL LOVE IT AND IT WILL CERTAINLY SHIVER YOUR TIMBERS.

SHIVER ME TIMBERS TILAPIA

WITH LAND LUBBER'S LEMON SAUCE

INGREDIENTS

    2 TILAPIA FILETS ABOUT 5-6 OUNCES EACH
    1 EGG
    1 TABLESPOON CORNSTARCH
    1/2 TEASPOON SALT
    1/4 TEASPOON PEPPER
    1 CUP BREADCRUMBS
    3 TABLESPOONS COOKING OIL

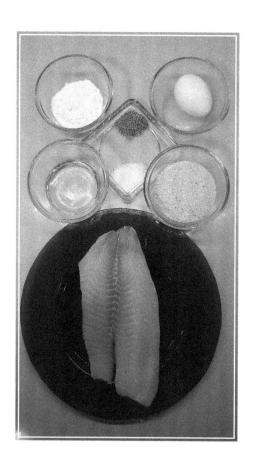

DIRECTIONS

1. IN A MEDIUM-SIZE SHALLOW BOWL, BEAT THE EGG WITH A FORK.
2. IN ANOTHER SHALLOW BOWL, MIX THE CORNSTARCH, SALT, AND PEPPER.
3. IN A THIRD SHALLOW BOWL, PUT IN THE BREADCRUMBS.
4. PLACE EACH TILAPIA FILET IN THE CORNSTARCH BOWL AND DUST BY TURNING THE FILET OVER ONCE SO BOTH SIDES ARE LIGHTLY COATED. DIP THE FILET INTO THE BOWL WITH THE EGG AND COAT IT. THEN MOVE IT TO THE BOWL WITH THE BREADCRUMBS AND DREDGE THE FISH GENEROUSLY TO COVER BOTH SIDES.
5. IN A MEDIUM-SIZE FRY PAN, HEAT THE OIL ON MEDIUM HIGH HEAT.
6. WHEN THE OIL IS GOOD AND HOT, YOU CAN PUT THE TILAPIA IN, AND COOK EACH SIDE UNTIL GOLDEN BROWN.
7. IF YOU WANT TO, YOU CAN MAKE THE LAND LUBBER'S LEMON SAUCE WHILE THE TILAPIA IS COOKING.

LAND LUBBER'S LEMON SAUCE

INGREDIENTS

- 1 LEMON JUICE AND ZEST
- 1 TEASPOON FINELY DICED GINGER
- 1/2 CUP WHITE WINE
- 1 TABLESPOON LEMON CURD
- 1/2 TEASPOON CORNSTARCH, MIXED WITH A LITTLE WATER
- 2 TABLESPOONS THINLY SLICED GREEN SCALLIONS

DIRECTIONS

1. IN A MEDIUM-SIZE SAUCEPAN ON MEDIUM HEAT, PUT THE LEMON JUICE AND ZEST, GINGER, WHITE WINE, AND LEMON CURD AND STIR UNTIL BUBBLY.
2. MIX THE CORNSTARCH WITH A LITTLE WATER, ADDING A WEE BIT AT A TIME WHILE CONSTANTLY STIRRING, AND THICKEN THE SAUCE TO YOUR SATISFACTION.
3. PLACE THE TILAPIA FILETS ON A PLATE AND LADLE LEMON SAUCE OVER THE FISH OR SERVE IT ON THE SIDE.

BEFORE SERVING SPRINKLE WITH THE SCALLIONS.

SHIVER ME TIMBERS TILAPIA

SHOWN WITH BRUSSELS SPROUTS AND POTATOES

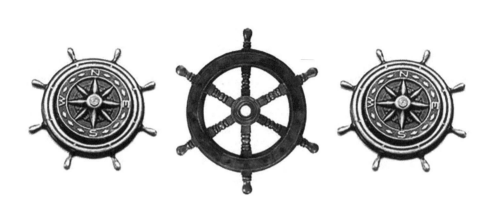

SANTA CATARINA ISLAND, BRAZIL

YOU'LL WALK THE PLANK FOR THIS NEXT DISH—THE EXOTIC COCO NELLA SHRIMP OF BRAZIL. WE FOUND A SPECIAL SPOT ON THE ISLAND OF SANTA CATARINA WHERE THE SHRIMP ARE MIGHTY A-PLENTY, AND WE PROUDLY SNATCH OUR SHARE.

WHILE WE CAPTURE THE HUGE MOUTHWATERING SHRIMP FROM THE TRANQUIL AQUAMARINE WATERS OF SANTA CATARINA, ONE-EYED WILLY WILL TAKE TOUCAN SALLY ON THE QUEST FOR THE FINEST AND FLAKIEST COCONUT FOR THIS SPECIAL COCO NELLA SHRIMP RECIPE. HE USES THE COCONUT TO COVER EACH DELECTABLE SHRIMP AND CARAMELIZES THEM TO A TOASTY BROWN DURING THE COOKING PROCESS. THE SAVORY SHRIMP IS ENCASED IN THE SWEET FLAVOR OF THE COCONUT. CRUSTY PIRATES SAY THESE COCO NELLAS TASTE FANTASTIC WITH THE PINEAPPLE PLUNDER SAUCE.

THIS COCONUT SHRIMP RECIPE IS SURE TO BECOME ONE OF YOUR VERY FAVORITES.

COCO NELLA SHRIMP

WITH PINEAPPLE PLUNDER SAUCE

INGREDIENTS

12 PIECES OF 16 TO 20 COUNT JUMBO SHRIMP—REMOVE SHELLS AND DEVEIN
1/2 CUP CORNSTARCH
2 EGGS
1 CUP FLAKED COCONUT
OIL TO DEEP FRY

DIRECTIONS

1. PUT THE SHRIMP INTO A LARGE PLASTIC BAG.
2. ADD THE CORNSTARCH TO THE BAG OF SHRIMP AND MIX AROUND TO COAT.
3. PUT THE EGGS INTO A MEDIUM-SIZE BOWL AND BEAT WITH A FORK.
4. PLACE EACH SHRIMP IN THE BOWL ONE AT A TIME TO COVER WITH THE EGG.
5. COAT EACH SHRIMP BY DREDGING IN THE COCONUT FLAKES.
6. REFRIGERATE FOR 30 MINUTES.
7. HEAT ENOUGH OIL TO SUBMERGE THE SHRIMP IN A DEEP FRYER OR MEDIUM POT AT 350 DEGREES. USE A COOKING THERMOMETER TO ENSURE TEMPERATURE.
8. PUT FIVE PIECES OF THE COATED SHRIMP AT A TIME. COOK UNTIL THE COCONUT TURNS GOLDEN BROWN.
9. SERVE WITH THE PINEAPPLE PLUNDER SAUCE.

PINEAPPLE PLUNDER SAUCE

INGREDIENTS

    8 OUNCES CRUSHED PINEAPPLE
    2 TABLESPOONS APRICOT JAM OR PRESERVES
    1 TABLESPOON RED CHILI FLAKE, USE MORE OR LESS AS YOU PREFER

DIRECTIONS

    MIX ALL INGREDIENTS IN A BOWL THOROUGHLY TO WARM YOUR BONES AND
SERVE.

COCONELLAS

SHOWN WITH BELL PEPPERS AND YELLOW RICE

CAMINO DEL NORTE, SPAIN

EUROPE IS ABOUT SIX THOUSAND MILES AWAY FROM SOUTH AMERICA, AND WE'RE IN IT FOR THE LONG HAUL. THERE ARE SO MANY INTRIGUING COUNTRIES AND COUNTLESS REGIONS, EACH WITH THEIR OWN LANGUAGE, CULTURE, AND DELIGHTFUL RECIPES!

IT'S A GOOD THING THE RELIABLE *AHOY MCCOY* IS VERY SPACIOUS AND WELL STOCKED WITH PLENTY OF DELICIOUS FOOD FOR OUR FANTASTIC VOYAGE. IN SOME WAYS, WE ARE THANKFUL FOR THE LONG SAIL BECAUSE ONE-EYED WILLY WILL HAVE PLENTY TIME TO COOK THESE FLAVORFUL RECIPES.

EVERY SAILOR IS BUSY DOING THEIR JOB, MAKING IT POSSIBLE TO SAFELY REACH OUR NEXT DESTINATION. AS CAPTAIN OF THIS VESSEL, I WILL BE DOWN IN MY STATE ROOM RELAXING.

FINALLY, AFTER MANY ROUGH DAYS AT SEA, WE REACH BEAUTIFUL CAMINO DEL NORTE, SPAIN, WITH ITS STUNNING COASTLINES, BREATHTAKING VIEWS, AND THE LEGENDARY PILGRIMAGE TRAIL.

PEOPLE HAVE TRAVELED UPON THIS TRAIL SINCE THE MIDDLE AGES. IT'S ABOUT FIVE HUNDRED MILES IN LENGTH, SO YOU CAN IMAGINE HOW LONG WE'VE HAD TO WAIT FOR ONE-EYED WILLY AND TOUCAN SALLY TO GET BACK TO THE SHIP AFTER GALLIVANTING ABOUT THE SPANISH TERRAIN, SUPPOSEDLY IN SEARCH OF THE FINEST PAPRIKA AROUND.

OUR FAVORITE MEAL IN THESE PARTS IS THE UNDENIABLY UNCONVENTIONAL SPANISH SCALLYWAG CHICKEN. IT INCLUDES A SPICY MEAT CALLED CHORIZO, WHICH HAS AN EXCEPTIONAL FLAVOR THAT IS WELL WORTH THE WAIT!

SPANISH SCALLYWAG CHICKEN

SPICE RUB INGREDIENTS

    2 TABLESPOONS OLIVE OIL
    1 TABLESPOON PAPRIKA
    1 TEASPOON CUMIN
    1 TEASPOON ONION POWDER
    1/4 TEASPOON OREGANO
    1/4 TEASPOON GARLIC SALT
    1/4 TEASPOON SALT
    1/4 TEASPOON PEPPER

CHICKEN INGREDIENTS

    2 BONELESS SKINLESS CHICKEN BREASTS
    3 TABLESPOONS OLIVE OIL
    9 OUNCE TUBE FINELY GROUND PORK OR BEEF CHORIZO
    14 OUNCES OF CHOPPED TOMATOES
    1 CUP CHICKEN STOCK
    1/2 A YELLOW ONION DICED
    5 CLOVES GARLIC DICED
    1/4 CUP DICED GREEN BELL PEPPER
    1/4 CUP DICED RED BELL PEPPER
    2 TABLESPOONS SLICED SCALLIONS

DIRECTIONS

1. IN A LARGE BOWL, MIX THE SPICES FOR THE RUB.
2. BUTTERFLY EACH CHICKEN BREAST BY CUTTING IT IN HALF LENGTH WISE.
3. IN ANOTHER LARGE BOWL, PUT 2 TABLESPOONS OF OLIVE OIL AND SLATHER THE CHICKEN BREASTS IN THE OIL. YOU CAN USE YOUR HANDS TO COMPLETELY COAT THE CHICKEN WITH THE OIL AND SPICES.
4. HEAT A MEDIUM-SIZE SKILLET ON MEDIUM HIGH HEAT. PUT IN THE CHORIZO AND STIR IT AROUND AS IT COOKS. COOK FOR 10-15 MINUTES UNTIL THOROUGHLY COOKED.
5. IN A MEDIUM-SIZE SKILLET ON MEDIUM HIGH HEAT, ADD 3 TABLESPOONS OF OIL. WHEN THE OIL IS HOT, PUT IN THE CHICKEN BREASTS AND COOK BOTH SIDES UNTIL THEY ARE WELL BROWNED. SET ASIDE IN A WARM OVEN.
6. IN THE SAME PAN, ADD THE ONIONS AND COOK UNTIL TRANSLUCENT.
7. ADD THE GARLIC AND COOK FOR 2 MINUTES.
8. ADD THE BELL PEPPERS AND COOK FOR ANOTHER 5 MINUTES.
9. ADD THE CHOPPED TOMATOES AND CHICKEN STOCK AND COOK FOR 5 MINUTES.
10. ADD THE COOKED CHORIZO AND COOK FOR FIVE MINUTES.
11. PUT THE CHICKEN BACK INTO THE PAN WITH THE SAUCE, COVER AND SIMMER FOR 15 MINUTES.
12. BEFORE SERVING SPRINKLE SCALLIONS ON TOP.

SCALLYWAG CHICKEN

SHOWN WITH BROCCOLI AND POTATOES

SANTA CRUZ, AZORES, PORTUGAL

Heading south, our journey is somewhat short from northwestern Spain to the tiny archipelago of Santa Cruz in the Azores. This group of nine volcanic islands is off the coast of Portugal, and word has it that this place has some of tallest mountains in all creation.

ME DEAR DEPARTED MOTHER, MARIE XAVIER, WAS BORN HERE IN SANTA CRUZ. HER NICKNAME WAS MAUDIE, AND SHE GREW UP HERE; BUT SOMEHOW, SHE ENDED UP IN CALIFORNIA. IT IS INDEED AN HONOR TO RETURN TO HER HOMELAND AND PAY RESPECTS. AFTER ALL, SHE IS THE WOMAN WHO GAVE ME THE PIRATE LIFE THAT I LOVE!

SHE WAS ALWAYS HAPPY TO MAKE HER FANTASTIC AZOREAN STYLE MAUDIE'S MARVELOUS MEATBALLS FEATURING PAPRIKA, THE TRADITIONAL PORTUGUESE SPICE. IT GIVES THE TENDER MEATBALLS A SPECIAL FLAVOR OF THE ISLANDS. TOUCAN SALLY SAYS IT TAKES TWO CANS OF ESSENTIAL TOMATO INGREDIENTS FOR THIS HANDED-DOWN RECIPE.

MY MOTHER'S OTHER SPECIALTY IS THE KILLER TWICE BEAN SALAD, ABUNDANT IN GARLIC, PARSLEY, AND PURPLE ONION. WE ARE USUALLY OUT TO SEA FOR WEEKS ON END; SO FLIES, MOSQUITOS, AND OTHER PESKY INSECTS WANT TO COME ALONG FOR THE RIDE. IT IS A HEALTH HAZARD INDEED. WE ARE RELIEVED TO HAVE FOUND THE PERFECT SOLUTION: RAW GARLIC, PARSLEY, AND PURPLE ONION! THESE INGREDIENTS ARE GOOD FOR YOU AND HAVE LIFESAVING PROPERTIES.

MAUDIE'S MARVELOUS MEATBALLS

INGREDIENTS

- 1 1/2 POUNDS GROUND BEEF
- 1 1/2 CUPS BREADCRUMBS
- 1 CUP DICED YELLOW ONION
- 2 EGGS
- 2 TABLESPOONS PORTUGUESE OR OTHER OLIVE OIL
- 1 TABLESPOON DRIED BASIL
- 1 TABLESPOON PAPRIKA
- 1 TEASPOON CUMIN
- 1 TEASPOON SALT
- 1 TEASPOON PEPPER

DIRECTIONS

1. IN A MEDIUM BOWL, MIX ALL THE INGREDIENTS TOGETHER EXCEPT THE OIL.
2. USE YOUR HANDS TO MAKE PALM-SIZED MEATBALLS.
3. IN A LARGE FRYING PAN, HEAT THE OIL ON MEDIUM HIGH AND COOK THE MEATBALLS UNTIL THEY ARE NICE AND BROWN. WHEN THEY ARE DONE, PUT THEM INTO AN OVEN AT LOW HEAT TO KEEP WARM.

MAUDIE'S AZOREAN MEATBALL SAUCE

INGREDIENTS

1 14-OUNCE CAN CRUSHED TOMATOES
1 14-OUNCE CAN TOMATO SAUCE
1/2 DICED YELLOW ONION
1/4 DICED RED BELL PEPPER
1/4 DICED GREEN BELL PEPPER
2 BAY LEAVES
1 TABLESPOON BASIL
1 TABLESPOON CUMIN
1 TABLESPOON PAPRIKA
1 TEASPOON SALT
1 TEASPOON BLACK PEPPER
1 TEASPOON WHITE PEPPER

DIRECTIONS

1. IN A MEDIUM SAUCEPAN, WARM 2 TABLESPOONS OLIVE OIL ON MEDIUM HIGH HEAT.
2. ADD THE ONIONS AND COOK FOR 5 MINUTES.
3. ADD THE BELL PEPPERS AND THE BAY LEAVES AND COOK FOR 3 MINUTES.
4. ADD ALL THE BASIL, CUMIN, PAPRIKA, SALT, BLACK PEPPER, AND WHITE PEPPER AND COOK FOR 3 MINUTES.
5. ADD THE TOMATO SAUCE AND THE CRUSHED TOMATOES, COOK UNTIL IT STARTS TO GET BUBBLY THEN TURN IT DOWN TO LOW AND SIMMER FOR 15 TO 20 MINUTES.
6. TAKE MEATBALLS FROM OVEN AND SERVE WITH THE SAUCE.

$\mathfrak{M}$ost pirates have heard of three bean salad, but this great recipe hails from Santa Cruz. Toucan Sally is glad to say that it takes two cans of legumes to make it taste just like mom would make.

KILLER TWICE BEAN SALAD

INGREDIENTS

1 16-ounce can kidney beans
1 16-ounce can chickpeas (garbanzo beans)
3/4 cup diced purple onion
3/4 cup red wine vinegar
1/4 cup Portuguese or other olive oil
2 tablespoons chopped fresh garlic
1 tablespoon chopped fresh parsley
1 tablespoon basil
1/4 teaspoon salt
1/2 teaspoon pepper

DIRECTIONS

Thoroughly mix all the ingredients in a medium-size bowl and chill for an hour in the refrigerator. Serve with the pride of a pirate.

MAUDIE'S MARVELOUS AZOREAN MEATBALLS AND KILLER TWICE BEAN

SHOWN WITH STEAMED BROCCOLI AND PASTA

MARSEILLE, FRANCE

FROM THE AZORES, WE BREEZE THROUGH THE STRAIT OF GIBRALTAR TO MARSEILLE--THE BIGGEST PORT IN FRANCE. FOR CENTURIES, SOAP HAS BEEN MADE HERE USING OLIVE OIL, SEA PLANTS, AND SEA WATER TO CREATE THE FAMOUS SAVON DE MARSEILLE, TREASURED FOR ITS PURITY AND QUALITY. WE MAKE SURE TO STOCK UP ON THIS FINE SOAP BECAUSE THE CREW MEMBERS ALL SMELL LIKE A FISH!

THERE ARE MANY KINDS OF LOCAL FISH HERE, BUT LEAVE IT TO ONE-EYED WILLY TO SAY, "LAND HO!" BECAUSE HE KNOWS OF A SPECIAL FARMER WHO RAISES CALVES IN THE AREA; AND OUR NEXT DISH FEATURES THIS TENDER MEAT CALLED VEAL. YOU WILL REALLY GOBBLE UP THESE VERY SOPHISTICATED VEAL CUTTHROAT CUTLETS.

WE POUND OUR MEAT AND COVER IT IN YE OLDE SPICED BREAD DUST, AND ONCE YOU'VE TASTED HOW FANTASTIC IT IS, YOU'LL WANT TO JUMP SHIP FOR MORE.

VEAL CUTTHROAT CUTLETS

INGREDIENTS

    4 THINLY SLICED VEAL PIECES CUT AS FOR SCALLOPINI
    2 TABLESPOONS CORNSTARCH
    1/2 TEASPOON SALT
    1/2 TEASPOON PEPPER
    1 1/2 CUPS BREADCRUMBS
    1 EGG
    4 TABLESPOONS COOKING OIL
    2 TABLESPOONS BUTTER

DIRECTIONS

1. PLACE EACH VEAL PIECE BETWEEN TWO PIECES OF PARCHMENT PAPER AND LIGHTLY POUND FOR TENDERNESS.
2. IN A MEDIUM-SIZE BOWL, MIX THE SALT, PEPPER, AND CORNSTARCH. DUST EACH PIECE OF VEAL PIECE WITH MIXTURE AND COAT THOROUGHLY.
3. IN ANOTHER MEDIUM-SIZE BOWL, WHISK THE EGGS, AND COAT THE VEAL.
4. IN YET ANOTHER BOWL, DREDGE THE VEAL WITH THE BREADCRUMBS.
5. IN A MEDIUM-SIZE FRY PAN, HEAT THE OIL ON MEDIUM HIGH HEAT.
6. WHEN THE OIL IS GOOD AND HOT, PLACE THE VEAL IN THE PAN AND COOK FOR 3 MINUTES.
7. TURN THEM OVER AND COOK FOR ANOTHER 3 MINUTES UNTIL NICELY BROWNED.
8. PLACE THE VEAL IN A WARM OVEN AND MAKE THE BUERRE BLANC SAUCE.

BUCCANEER BUERRE BLANC SAUCE

INGREDIENTS

- 1 CUP COLD UNSALTED BUTTER, CUT INTO SMALL SQUARES
- 4 TABLESPOONS DRY WHITE WINE
- 2 TABLESPOONS FRESH LEMON JUICE
- 2 TABLESPOONS HEAVY CREAM
- 1 FINELY CHOPPED SHALLOT
- 1 TABLESPOON CHOPPED FRESH PARSLEY
- 1/4 TEASPOON SALT

DIRECTIONS

1. IN A MEDIUM SAUCEPAN ON MEDIUM HIGH HEAT, ADD THE SHALLOTS AND WINE AND COOK UNTIL ALL THE LIQUID HAS REDUCED TO ALMOST NOTHING.
2. ADD THE HEAVY CREAM AND SIMMER FOR 3 MINUTES BUT DON'T LET IT BOIL.
3. TURN THE HEAT DOWN TO LOW AND STIR IN THE LEMON JUICE.
4. START ADDING THE BUTTER A COUPLE PIECES AT A TIME WHILE SLOWLY STIRRING USING A WHISK TO HELP MELT THE BUTTER. ADD THE OTHER PIECES OF BUTTER UNTIL ALL THE BUTTER HAS MELTED.

SERVE IMMEDIATELY

THE SAUCE WON'T BE ANY GOOD IF IT SITS AROUND AND GETS COLD
SO POUR THE BEURRE BLANC OVER THE VEAL OR SERVE IT ON THE SIDE

VEAL CUTTHROAT IN BUCCANEER BEURRE BLANC SAUCE

SHOWN WITH GREEN BEANS AND ABOUT THYME RED POTATOES

MARSALA, SICILY, ITALY

THE PLEASANT JOURNEY ON THE TURQUOISE SEAS FROM MARSEILLE TO MARSALA IS ALWAYS A BREEZE. YOU CAN SEE THE ISLAND OF SARDINIA AS WE SAIL SOUTHEAST TO SICILY, THE LARGEST ISLAND IN THE MEDITERRANEAN. SICILY IS A TRIANGULAR SHAPED ISLAND, AND FROM OUR TREASURE MAP, IT LOOKS LIKE THE BOOT OF ITALY IS KICKING IT.

IT'S EASY TO UNDERSTAND WHY OUR MARSALA PIRATE FOWL RECIPE IS IRRESISTIBLE. IT FEATURES MARSALA, WHICH IS AN AROMATIC RAISIN WINE THAT WAS CREATED RIGHT HERE IN THE TOWN OF MARSALA, SICILY! ONE-EYED WILLY PURLOINED A BARREL, I MEAN RECEIVED A BARREL OF THIS COVETED MARSALA WINE, SO HELP YOURSELF TO AS MUCH AS YOU WISH.

ONE-EYED WILLY IS ALSO IN ACQUAINTANCE OF A LOCAL DAIRY FARMER WHO HAS THE FINEST FRESH CREAM IN ALL THE LAND. THIS FARMER ALSO HAS LOTS OF CHICKENS, AND HE AND TOUCAN SALLY WILL MOST LIKELY RETURN TO THE SHIP WITH A FEW CAGES OF CHICKENS. WE WILL ALWAYS NEED EGGS; AND WE DO EAT A LOT OF CHICKEN, SO ALL ABOARD!

YOU AAARRRRRGH IN FOR A REAL TREAT WITH THIS AWESOME DISH MADE WITH THE HERALDED MAAAARRRRRSALA WINE FROM MARSALA!

MARSALA PIRATE FOWL

INGREDIENTS

2 BONELESS SKINLESS CHICKEN BREASTS
1/2 CUP FLOUR
1 TEASPOON SALT
1 TEASPOON PEPPER
3 TABLESPOONS VEGETABLE OIL
2 TABLESPOONS BUTTER
2 PIECES OF PARCHMENT PAPER

DIRECTIONS

1. BUTTERFLY EACH CHICKEN BREAST BY CUTTING IT IN HALF LENGTHWISE.
2. PUT BREASTS BETWEEN THE TWO PIECES OF PARCHMENT PAPER AND POUND WITH A MALLET OR USE A ROLLING PIN UNTIL THE CHICKEN IS EVENLY FLAT.
3. IN A SHALLOW BOWL, MIX TOGETHER THE FLOUR, SALT, AND PEPPER.
4. DREDGE EACH BREAST IN THE FLOUR MIXTURE UNTIL FULLY COATED.
5. IN A MEDIUM SAUCEPAN, HEAT THE OIL AND BUTTER UNTIL BUBBLY.
6. ADD THE CHICKEN AND COOK ON MEDIUM HIGH HEAT FOR 3 TO 4 MINUTES OR UNTIL GOLDEN BROWN. SET THEM ON A COOKIE SHEET IN A WARM OVEN.

MARSALA PIRATE SAUCE

INGREDIENTS

1/4 CUP OLIVE OIL
1 LARGE SHALLOT, DICED
2 CUPS OF YOUR FAVORITE MUSHROOMS
2 CLOVES DICED GARLIC
1 CUP MARSALA WINE
1 CUP CHICKEN STOCK
SALT AND PEPPER TO YOUR TASTE
2 TABLESPOONS BUTTER AND OPTIONAL EXTRA BUTTER TO THICKEN
1 TABLESPOON CHOPPED FRESH PARSLEY
1 TABLESPOON CHOPPED FRESH THYME

DIRECTIONS

1. IN THE SAME PAN THAT THE CHICKEN WAS COOKED IN, PUT THE OLIVE OIL AND SHALLOTS AND COOK FOR 3 MINUTES.
2. ADD THE MUSHROOMS AND GARLIC AND COOK FOR 5 MINUTES.
3. POUR IN THE MARSALA TO DEGLAZE THE PAN. IT WILL MAKE A LOT OF NOISE AND CAUSE SOME STEAM WHEN IT HITS THE PAN. USE A SPATULA TO SCRAPE ALL THE TASTY BITS ON THE BOTTOM OF THE PAN, AND MIX THOROUGHLY.
4. BRING TO A LOW BOIL AND ADD THE CHICKEN STOCK, SALT, AND PEPPER. AS IT STARTS TO BOIL AGAIN, ADD THE BUTTER A LITTLE BIT AT A TIME. WHEN ALL THE BUTTER HAS MELTED, LET SIMMER FOR 10 MINUTES, AND THE SAUCE WILL THICKEN.
5. PLACE THE COOKED CHICKEN BACK INTO THE PAN WITH THE SAUCE AND SIMMER FOR 3 MINUTES.

WHEN READY TO SERVE, POUR THE SAUCE OVER THE CHICKEN
AND SPRINKLE THE PARSLEY AND THYME ON TOP AND ENJOY!

MARSALA PIRATE FOWL

SHOWN WITH MULTI-COLORED CARROTS AND MASHED POTATOES WITH CAPERS

ATHENS, GREECE

We GLIDE AROUND THE BOOT OF ITALY ON THE PEACEFUL IONIAN SEA TO OUR NEXT EXCITING STOP, ATHENS, GREECE.

GOOD THING THAT ONE-EYED WILLY KNOWS WHERE TO STEAL, I MEAN BARTER FOR THE IMPORTANT INGREDIENTS IN OUR NEXT BOUNTY O' GOODS: THE STUFFED CHICKEN OF THE GODS. HE AND TOUCAN SALLY HAVE VENTURED THIS TRIP NUMEROUS TIMES, AND THEY HAVE MADE MANY FRIENDS HERE. GREECE IS KNOWN FOR ITS SALTY MILD FETA CHEESE AND CRUNCHY WALNUTS. GREEKS ALSO USE A LOT OF CUCUMBER, AND ONE-EYED WILLY KNOWS JUST WHERE TO GET THE FRESHEST IN ALL THE LAND. HE ENJOYS GETTING CREATIVE AND TURNS THE CUCUMBERS INTO ARTISTIC MASTERPIECES.

STUFFED CHICKEN OF THE GODS

INGREDIENTS

- 2 BONELESS AND SKINNED CHICKEN BREAST
- 4 TABLESPOONS FETA CHEESE
- 2 TABLESPOONS CHOPPED WALNUTS
- 1 TABLESPOON CHOPPED FRESH PARSLEY
- 1/2 TEASPOON SALT
- 1/2 TEASPOON PEPPER
- 1/3 CUP CORNSTARCH
- 2 EGGS
- 2 CUPS BREADCRUMBS
- 1/2 CUP VEGETABLE OIL
- 3 TABLESPOONS BUTTER

DIRECTIONS

1. SLICE EACH CHICKEN BREAST LENGTHWISE TO CREATE A POCKET.
2. MIX THE FETA, WALNUTS, AND PARSLEY TOGETHER AND STUFF EACH BREAST WITH AS MUCH OF THE MIXTURE AS YOU CAN. AND WHEN FULLY STUFFED, PINCH THE OPENING WITH YOUR FINGERS TO CLOSE THE SLIT. DO NOT LICK FINGERS AFTER TOUCHING RAW CHICKEN.
3. MIX THE SALT AND PEPPER IN THE CORNSTARCH AND DUST THE BREASTS WITH THE CORNSTARCH MIXTURE.
4. IN A SHALLOW BOWL, WHISK THE EGGS AND THEN DRAG THE CHICKEN THROUGH THE EGG TO COAT IT.
5. PUT THE BREADCRUMBS IN ANOTHER SHALLOW BOWL AND DREDGE THE STUFFED CHICKEN TO THOROUGHLY COAT IT.
6. IN A MEDIUM-SIZE SAUCEPAN, HEAT THE OIL AND BUTTER ON MEDIUM HIGH HEAT.
7. PUT THE CHICKEN IN AND COOK BOTH SIDES TO A GOLDEN BROWN.
8. PUT THEM IN THE OVEN ON A COOKIE SHEET AT 350 DEGREES FOR 20 MINUTES. MAKE SURE THE INTERNAL TEMPERATURE OF THE CHICKEN IS AT LEAST 160 DEGREES.

SERVE WITH THE VELVETY IT'S ALL GREEK TO ME SAUCE.

IT'S ALL GREEK TO ME SAUCE

INGREDIENTS

    4 TABLESPOONS LEMON JUICE
    1/2 CUP HEAVY CREAM
    3/4 CUP MARSALA WINE
    1 TABLESPOON BUTTER

DIRECTIONS

1. IN THE SAME PAN THAT THE CHICKEN WAS COOKED IN, SPOON OUT MOST OF THE COOKING OIL BUT NOT THE LITTLE CRUMB BITS ON THE BOTTOM OF THE PAN.
2. HEAT THE PAN TO MEDIUM HIGH. POUR IN THE MARSALA AND LEMON JUICE. BEWARE, IT'LL GET NOISY AND STEAMY AS YOU DEGLAZE THE BOTTOM OF THE PAN BY ADDING THE LIQUIDS. SCRAPE UP ALL THE LITTLE BITS AND SWIRL AROUND.
3. WHEN IT BEGINS TO LIGHTLY BOIL, TURN THE HEAT DOWN AND SLOWLY STIR IN THE HEAVY CREAM.
4. ADD THE BUTTER TO THICKEN THE SAUCE AND COOK ON LOW FOR 5 MINUTES.

POUR THE SAUCE OVER CHICKEN OR SERVE IT ON THE SIDE

STUFFED CHICKEN OF THE GODS WITH
IT'S ALL GREEK TO ME SAUCE

SHOWN WITH ASPARAGUS AND POTATOES WITH CARAMELIZED PURPLE ONION

MINICOY ISLAND, INDIA

WE SAIL ANOTHER LONG JOURNEY ON THE STEADFAST *AHOY MCCOY*, TRAVELING FROM GREECE ALL THE WAY TO MINICOY ISLAND IN AN ARCHIPELAGO OFF INDIA'S FAMED SOUTHWEST COAST. IT IS SMOOTH SAILING, WHICH IS GOOD BECAUSE THE CREW IS GOING CRAZY WITH ALL THE CLUCKING CHICKENS THAT ONE-EYED WILLY GOT A WHILE BACK. THESE NOISY BIRDS ARE KEEPING THE CREW AWAKE AT NIGHT, AND WE NEED A WELL-RESTED CREW TO ACCOMPLISH THE MANY IMPORTANT DUTIES WE HAVE ABOARD SHIP SUCH AS COLLECTING ALL THE CACKLEBERRIES AND CLEANING THAT DARN CHICKEN COOP.

THOSE RASCALS, ONE-EYED WILLY AND TOUCAN SALLY, ARE NOWHERE TO BE SEEN BECAUSE THEY PROBABLY TREKKED TO THEIR FRIEND'S PLACE FOR THE BEST SPICES IN ALL THE LAND.

$\mathfrak{I}$T'S TRUE WE ALSO NEED A WELL-NOURISHED CREW, AND THIS GOOD KARMA CHICKEN RECIPE IS ONE OF THEIR FAVORITES. IT WILL TANTALIZE YOUR TASTE BUDS WITH DELIGHTFUL SPICY FLAVORS THAT SWIRL AND DANCE ON YOUR TONGUE.

IT IS SO TERRIFIC THAT YOU WILL WANT TO PUT YOUR FORK DOWN ON THE TABLE, PUT YOUR HANDS IN THE AIR AND YELL, "STOP THE MEAL! IT'S TOO GOOD TO EAT!"

GOOD KARMA CHICKEN

INGREDIENTS

- 2 BONELESS SKINLESS CHICKEN BREASTS, CUT INTO BITE-SIZE PIECES
- 4 TABLESPOONS BUTTER
- 5 CLOVES DICED GARLIC
- 1 TABLESPOON FINELY CHOPPED FRESH GINGER
- 1 SMALL THINLY SLICED YELLOW ONION
- 1 TEASPOON CORIANDER
- 1 TEASPOON CUMIN
- 1 TEASPOON RED PEPPER CHILI FLAKES
- 4 TABLESPOONS VERY FINELY CHOPPED ALMONDS
- 1/2 TEASPOON CINNAMON
- 1/2 TEASPOON CLOVES
- 2 TEASPOONS TURMERIC
- 1/4 TEASPOON SALT
- 1/4 TEASPOON PEPPER
- 1 CUP PLAIN YOGURT
- 1 TABLESPOON LEMON JUICE
- 1 TABLESPOON CHOPPED FRESH PARSLEY
- 2 TABLESPOONS CHOPPED FRESH CILANTRO

DIRECTIONS

1. IN A MEDIUM-SIZE, SKILLET MELT THE BUTTER OVER MEDIUM HIGH HEAT.
2. ADD GARLIC, GINGER, AND ONION AND COOK UNTIL THE ONION IS TRANSLUCENT.
3. ADD CORIANDER, CUMIN, AND CHILI FLAKES. COOK FOR 3 MINUTES.
4. ADD THE CHICKEN AND COOK UNTIL THE CHICKEN IS NO LONGER PINK.
5. ADD THE ALMONDS, CINNAMON, CLOVES, TURMERIC, SALT, AND PEPPER, MIXING THOROUGHLY WHILE COOKING ANOTHER 3 MINUTES.
6. ADD THE YOGURT AND SLOWLY BLEND IT ALL TOGETHER.
7. COVER THE PAN WITH A LID, REDUCE HEAT, AND SIMMER FOR 45 MINUTES, STIRRING OCCASIONALLY.

BEFORE SERVING SPRINKLE WITH
LEMON JUICE, CHOPPED PARSLEY, AND CILANTRO.

GOOD KARMA CHICKEN

SHOWN WITH PETITE PEAS AND COUSCOUS

SINGAPORE

WE NOW TRAVEL TO EXOTIC SINGAPORE, JUST ONE DEGREE NORTH OF THE EQUATOR. THERE ARE COUNTLESS ISLANDS TO CHOOSE FROM, AND WE LIKE TO EXPERIMENT WITH AS MANY OF THEIR DIFFERENT DELICIOUS CUISINES AS POSSIBLE.

ONE OF OUR FAVORITE DISHES FROM THESE WATERS IS THE SAVE YOURSELF FROM SCURVY MALAYSIAN ORANGE CHICKEN. THE ORANGES ARE PACKED WITH LOTS OF VITAMIN C TO KEEP THE DREADED SCURVY AWAY. THE PAPRIKA AND WHITE PEPPER GIVE IT A LITTLE KICK; AND THESE SPICES ARE CONTRASTED BY THE FLAVORFUL SWEET RAISINS, SO PLUMP WITH THE MADEIRA WINE THEY JUICILY BURST IN YOUR MOUTH BY SURPRISE.

ONE-EYED WILLY AND TOUCAN SALLY SAY THAT DRINKING THE MADEIRA MAY HORNSWAGGLE YOUR SENSES, AND YOU COULD BE THREE SHEETS TO THE WIND IF YOU HAVE TOO MUCH.

IT IS OBVIOUS TO US THAT THOSE TWO WILL GET SIDETRACKED, AND THEY'LL WANDER OFF TO MEET YET ANOTHER FRIEND WHO HAS THE SWEETEST TINY ORANGES IN ALL THE LAND. WE NEVER KNOW HOW LONG THEY WILL BE GONE OR WHERE THEY ARE GOING OR WHEN THEY'LL BE BACK. WE'LL MAKE THE BEST OF IT AND ENJOY THE NICE WEATHER AND CALM SHORES. MOST IMPORTANTLY, WHEN THEY FINALLY DO RETURN, WE ABSOLUTELY MUST KNOW WHETHER THEY ARE WITH OR WITHOUT THE PRECIOUS MADEIRA. IT REALLY MATTERS.

SAVE YOURSELF FROM SCURVY
MALAYSIAN ORANGE CHICKEN

INGREDIENTS

2 SKINNED BONELESS CHICKEN BREASTS, CUT INTO SMALL CUBES
3 TABLESPOONS WHITE RAISINS
1/2 CUP MADEIRA WINE
2 TABLESPOONS PAPRIKA
1 TABLESPOON WHITE PEPPER
6 TABLESPOONS VEGETABLE OIL
1 15 OUNCE CAN MANDARIN ORANGES (RESERVE THE JUICE)
3 CLOVES DICED GARLIC
1/2 CUP CHICKEN STOCK
1 TABLESPOON SOY SAUCE
1 TEASPOON FINELY CHOPPED FRESH GINGER
1 TABLESPOON CORNSTARCH
1 TABLESPOON BUTTER
3 TABLESPOONS SLICED ALMONDS
½ CUP HEAVY LIQUID WHIPPING CREAM

DIRECTIONS

1. PUT THE RAISINS AND MADEIRA IN A SMALL BOWL, MAKING SURE THAT ALL THE RAISINS ARE SUBMERGED. SET ASIDE.
2. IN A MEDIUM ZIP LOCK BAG, MIX THE PAPRIKA AND WHITE PEPPER. PUT THE CHICKEN IN THE BAG AND SHAKE IT AROUND AND THOROUGHLY COAT EACH PIECE.
3. HEAT THE OIL ON A MEDIUM TO LARGE SKILLET AND ADD THE CHICKEN AND COOK FOR ABOUT TEN MINUTES AND COOK TO A GOLDEN BROWN.
4. POUR THE JUICE FROM THE MANDARIN ORANGES INTO THE PAN AND ADD THE GARLIC AND CHICKEN STOCK. REDUCE HEAT AND SIMMER FOR 30 MINUTES.
5. ADD THE SOY SAUCE AND GINGER AND MIX WELL.
6. POUR OFF THE MADEIRA FROM THE RAISINS AND ADD THE RAISINS TO THE PAN, AND COOK FOR 3 MINUTES.

7. PUT THE CORNSTARCH IN A SMALL BOWL AND ADD A SMALL AMOUNT OF WATER AND STIR UNTIL COMPLETELY BLENDED. AS THE SAUCE GETS BUBBLY, SLOWLY ADD THE CORNSTARCH A LITTLE BIT AT A TIME WHILE STIRRING TO THICKEN THE SAUCE TO YOUR LIKING.
8. IN A SMALL FRY PAN MELT THE BUTTER ON MEDIUM HEAT.
9. ADD THE ALMONDS AND STIR CONTINUOUSLY UNTIL THE ALMONDS ARE LIGHT BROWN. IN GENERAL, NUTS WILL CONTINUE TO COOK AFTER THEY COME OFF THE HEAT, SO TAKE THAT INTO CONSIDERATION AND DON'T BURN 'EM. SET ASIDE.
10. SLOWLY ADD THE CREAM TO THE CHICKEN PAN AND BLEND WELL.
11. TURN OFF THE HEAT AND ADD THE ORANGES. GENTLY STIR ONLY ONCE BECAUSE THE ORANGES ARE VERY FRAGILE AND CANNOT WITHSTAND TOO MUCH HEAT OR DISRUPTION.
12. SERVE IMMEDIATELY WITH A SPRINKLE OF THE TOASTY ALMONDS ON TOP.

SAVE YOURSELF FROM
SCURVY MALAYSIAN ORANGE CHICKEN

SHOWN HERE WITH SNOW PEAS AND BLACK SESAME SEEDED BASMATI RICE

HONG KONG, CHINA

We ARE BACK ABOARD THE *AHOY MCCOY* AND HEADED NORTH ON THE SOUTH CHINA SEA, SAILING ABOUT 1,500 MILES TO THE FRAGRANT HARBOR OF HONG KONG. WE HAVEN'T BEEN HERE IN AGES, SO IT IS NICE TO RETURN TO ASIA'S GLORIOUS WORLD CITY AND TAKE IT ALL IN. THE VAST AMOUNTS OF SO MANY DELICIOUS AROMAS BLOW ABOARD AROUND HERE AND CAN BE OVERWHELMING, SO STAY EVEN KEELED.

IT IS A KNOWN FACT THAT ONE-EYED WILLY WILL TRAIPSE OFF WITH TOUCAN SALLY TO MEET LONG-TIME FRIENDS THAT HAVE THE FINEST CASHEWS IN ALL THE LAND. WE CAN'T WAIT FOR THEM TO GET BACK TO THE AHOY MCCOY AND MAKE US ONE OF OUR FAVORITE PLATES CALLED KING POW CHIN-CHIN.

THE BLACKENING OF THE CHILIES CREATES A VERY DISTINCT SMELL THAT WILL FILL YOUR SAILS LIKE NO OTHER. ARE YOU READY TO RIDE THE DRAGON? NEXT WILL COME A TOASTY WHIFF OF THE CASHEWS AS YOU PREPARE THEM FOR THIS DISH THAT IS ABSOLUTE HEAVEN OF THE SEA ON EARTH! IT MIGHT HAVE YOU SAYING, "OH WOW," AND "POW TO THE KING!"

KING POW CHIN-CHIN

INGREDIENTS

PHASE 1: THE MARINADE

2 BONELESS SKINLESS CHICKEN BREASTS
2 TABLESPOONS SHERRY WINE
2 TABLESPOONS SOY SAUCE
1 TEASPOONS CORNSTARCH

PHASE 2: THE SAUCE

2 TABLESPOONS CHICKEN BROTH
2 TABLESPOONS SHERRY WINE
2 TABLESPOONS SOY SAUCE
1 TABLESPOON RICE WINE VINEGAR
1 TEASPOON CORNSTARCH
1/3 TEASPOON SUGAR

THE REST OF THE INGREDIENTS

2 TABLESPOONS COOKING OIL
4 TO 5 DRIED WHOLE RED CHILIES
1/4 CUP CASHEW NUTS
1 1/2 TEASPOON FRESH GINGER
1/4 CUP RED BELL PEPPERS
1/4 CUP YELLOW BELL PEPPERS
1/4 CUP PURPLE ONION

DIRECTIONS

1. CUT THE CHICKEN INTO ONE-INCH BITE-SIZE PIECES AND PUT IN A LARGE BOWL.

2. MARINADE: ADD 2 TABLESPOONS SHERRY, 2 TABLESPOONS SOY SAUCE, AND 1 TEASPOON CORNSTARCH AND MIX WELL WITH THE CHICKEN AND SET ASIDE.

3. SAUCE: IN A SMALL BOWL, COMBINE 2 TABLESPOONS OF CHICKEN BROTH, 2 TABLESPOONS SHERRY, 2 TABLESPOONS SOY SAUCE, 1 TABLESPOON RICE WINE VINEGAR, 1 TEASPOON CORNSTARCH, AND 1/4 TEASPOON SUGAR. SET ASIDE.

4. IN A MEDIUM TO LARGE SKILLET, HEAT THE TWO TABLESPOONS OF COOKING OIL OVER MEDIUM HIGH HEAT.

5. ADD THE RED CHILIES; AND COOK UNTIL THEY ARE ALMOST BLACK AND REMOVE THEM FROM THE PAN.

6. ADD THE CASHEW NUTS UNTIL THEY ARE LIGHTLY BROWNED THEN REMOVE THEM FROM THE PAN. THE NUTS WILL COOK EVEN AFTER YOU REMOVE THEM FROM THE PAN SO TAKE THEM OUT WHEN THEY ARE SLIGHTLY BROWNED, OR THEY MAY BURN.

7. ON THE SAME HEAT IN THE SAME PAN WITH THE OIL THAT IS NOW INFUSED WITH THE CHILI FLAVOR, ADD THE CHICKEN ALONG WITH THE MARINADE MIXTURE AND COOK 5 MINUTES, MAKING SURE THE CHICKEN IS NO LONGER PINK.
8. ADD THE GINGER, BELL PEPPERS, AND ONION AND COOK 5 MINUTES.
9. ADD THE SAUCE TO THE PAN AND COOK 5 MINUTES.
10. BRING TO A LOW BOIL AND SIMMER 5 MINUTES.
11. ADD THE CASHEW NUTS AND RED CHILIES AND COOK ANOTHER 3 MINUTES

KING POW CHIN-CHIN

SHOWN HERE WITH WHITE RICE AND STEAMED BABY CORN AND DOLPHIN PEAS

SHANGHAI, CHINA

LEAVING THE HARBOR OF HONG KONG, THE *AHOY MCCOY* GENTLY FLOATS US FASTER THAN AN IRISH HURRICANE ABOUT 660 NAUTICAL MILES NORTH ON THE EAST CHINA SEA. ONE-ARMED LEFTY STILL DOESN'T UNDERSTAND HOW WE CAN TRAVEL NORTH WHEN IT IS CALLED THE EAST CHINA SEA.

OUR NEXT EXCITING DESTINATION IS THE PEARL OF ASIA——THE ONE AND ONLY SHANGRI-LA THAT IS KNOWN AS SHANGHAI. SO LONG AS WE DON'T GET SHANG-HAIED, WE'LL BE JUST FINE.

IT WILL BE BUSINESS AS USUAL FOR ONE-EYED WILLY AND TOUCAN SALLY AS THEY WILL HEAD OUT AT DAYBREAK ON A MISSION TO COURSE THE LONG ROUTE TO A LOCAL FRIEND'S FARM TO LASSO THE VERY BEST LITTLE PIGGY IN ALL THE LAND. THIS RECIPE OF SWEET AND SOUR SWINE HAS A TANGY GOODNESS THAT WILL MAKE YOU SQUEAL FOR MORE!

IN FACT, IT IS SO GOOD THAT IT WILL TURN ANY SEA-LOVING SAILOR INTO A PORK-LOVING SHOREBIRD.

SHANGHAI SHIP SHAPE SWEET AND SOUR SWINE

INGREDIENTS

PHASE 1: THE SWEET AND SOUR SAUCE

1/3 CUP RICE VINEGAR
4 TABLESPOONS BROWN SUGAR
1 TABLESPOON OF CATSUP
1 TABLESPOON OF SOY SAUCE
4 TEASPOONS OF WATER
1 TEASPOONS OF CORN STARCH
1/2 TEASPOON OF FRESH GINGER

DIRECTIONS

IN A SMALL SAUCEPAN ON MEDIUM HEAT, MIX ALL OF THE SAUCE INGREDIENTS AND BRING TO A ROLLING BOIL. SIMMER UNTIL YOU ARE SATISFIED WITH THE THICKNESS OF THE SAUCE.

PHASE 2: THE SWINE INGREDIENTS

1 1/2 POUNDS PORK LOIN, CUT INTO BITE-SIZE PIECES
1/2 ONION, CUT INTO WIDE SLIVERS
1/2 OF A YELLOW BELL PEPPER AND 1/2 OF AN ORANGE BELL PEPPER, BOTH
    CUT INTO LENGTHS AND THEN CUT IN HALF
1/2 CUP PINEAPPLE CHUNKS
1/2 CUP PINEAPPLE JUICE
1 TABLESPOON SESAME SEEDS
3 TABLESPOONS COOKING OIL

SHIP SHAPE SWEET AND SOUR SWINE

DIRECTIONS

1. IN A LARGE FRY PAN, HEAT THE OIL ON MEDIUM HIGH HEAT.
2. ADD THE PORK AND COOK 7 MINUTES.
3. ADD THE ONION AND BELL PEPPERS AND COOK 4 MINUTES.
4. ADD THE SWEET AND SOUR SAUCE MIXTURE, PINEAPPLE CHUNKS, AND THE PINEAPPLE JUICE. COOK FOR 3 MINUTES OR UNTIL THE SAUCE THICKENS TO YOUR DESIRE.

BEFORE SERVING, SPRINKLE WITH SESAME SEEDS.

SHIP SHAPE SWEET AND SOUR SWINE

SHOWN WITH BOK CHOY AND WHITE RICE

HOKKAIDO, JAPAN

The fantastic smells wafting onto the *AHOY MCCOY* guide us to Hokkaido, the second largest island in Japan. We must plan the timing of our visit very carefully as this area has some of the most snow in the world. The cold Siberian wind across the warm ocean water can cause snow to produce, even without a storm. You can probably imagine that the snow can be a real setback for us, and the crew gets cranky and unruly when they are below deck for too long.

One-eyed Willy always takes Toucan Sally to the famous Hokkaido Pork and Strawberry Festival even though we already have plenty of pork. She likes to taste the renowned strawberries and see all the brilliant flowers that are in bloom at this time of year.

WE ALL KNOW WHAT HAPPENED THE LAST TIME WE CAME THROUGH HERE WHEN THEY WENT SCAVENGING, SO THEY'LL PROBABLY GET WAYLAID AND END UP IN SAPPORO, HOKKAIDO'S CAPITAL CITY. WHO CAN BLAME THEM FOR WANTING TO GET A FRESH TASTE OF THE FAMOUS TIME-TESTED BEER? IT HAS BEEN RESPECTFULLY BREWED HERE SINCE 1877 AND ME THINKS THE SPACIOUS *AHOY MCCOY* HAS PLENTY OF ROOM TO TAKE SOME OF THE BREW INTO STORAGE.

WE STILL HAVE A FEW NOISY CHICKENS THAT NEED TO TAKE A LONG WALK ON A SHORT PIER SO WE WILL ALL ENJOY SAVORING THIS NEXT STUNNINGLY YUMMY RECIPE CALLED TERIYUMI CHICKEN. IT IS OUR UNTRADITIONAL PIRATE VERSION OF TERIYAKI CHICKEN. WE KNOW YOU'RE GOING TO LOVE IT!

TERIYUMI CHICKEN

TERIYUMI SAUCE INGREDIENTS

    1 CUP WATER
    1/2 CUP SOY SAUCE
    3 TABLESPOONS BROWN SUGAR
    1 CLOVES OF GRATED GARLIC
    1/2 TEASPOONS OF GRATED FRESH GINGER
    2 TABLESPOONS HONEY
    2 TABLESPOONS SESAME SEEDS
    2 TABLESPOONS OF CORNSTARCH
    1 TABLESPOON OF SESAME OIL

TERIYUMI SAUCE DIRECTIONS

1. IN A MEDIUM SAUCEPAN, MIX ALL THE INGREDIENTS EXCEPT THE CORN-STARCH ON MEDIUM HEAT AND BRING IT TO A LOW BOIL.
2. MIX THE CORNSTARCH WITH A LITTLE WATER AND ADD A WEE BIT AT A TIME WHILE CONSTANTLY STIRRING AND THICKEN THE SAUCE TO YOUR SAT-ISFACTION. KEEP IT WARM ON LOW AND STIR EVERY NOW AND THEN.

TERIYUMI CHICKEN INGREDIENTS

1/2 CUP BITE-SIZE PIECES RED BELL PEPPER
1/2 CUP BITE-SIZE PIECES GREEN BELL PEPPER
1/2 CUP SLICED YELLOW ONION
2 CHICKEN BREASTS, CUT INTO BITE-SIZE PIECES
2 GREEN ONIONS, CUT DIAGONALLY IN ONE-INCH LENGTHS
2 CLOVES OF GARLIC, DICED
3 TABLESPOONS COOKING OIL

TERIYUMI CHICKEN DIRECTIONS

1. IN A LARGE FRY PAN, HEAT THE OIL ON MEDIUM HEAT.
2. ADD THE ONION AND COOK UNTIL TRANSLUCENT.
3. ADD THE BELL PEPPERS AND COOK FOR 3 MINUTES.
4. ADD THE GARLIC AND COOK FOR 2 MINUTES.
5. ADD THE CHICKEN AND COOK UNTIL IT IS NO LONGER PINK.
6. GENTLY POUR THE TERIYUMI SAUCE OVER THE CHICKEN. BRING TO A LOW BUBBLY BOIL AND SIMMER FOR 5 MINUTES.
7. BEFORE SERVING, SPRINKLE WITH THE GREEN ONION.

TERIYUMI CHICKEN

SHOWN HERE WITH FORBIDDEN CARROTS AND HERBED RICE

KODIAK, ALASKA

WE RELUCTANTLY DEPART ENCHANTING ASIA AND NAVIGATE NORTH-EAST ON THE FAMILIAR BIG BLUE PACIFIC OCEAN. WE'LL KNOW WHEN WE ARE GETTING CLOSE TO OUR NEXT FABULOUS DESTINATION WHEN WE SEE THE ALEUTIAN ISLANDS, ONE OF ALASKA'S MANY ARCHIPELAGOS. FROM HERE, IT IS ONLY ABOUT 900 MILES TO KODIAK ISLAND, FAMED FOR BEING INFESTED WITH HUGE KODIAK BEARS. KODIAK BEARS ARE A SUBSPECIES OF BROWN BEAR, AND THEY HAVE LIVED HERE FOR OVER 12,000 YEARS. I FEEL A CHAL-LENGE AND I AM UP FOR IT!

SALMON IS THE LIFEBLOOD OF THE FOOD IN ALASKA. WELL, IT IS ALSO A FAVORITE OF THESE DEADLY BEARS. THIS WILD TUNDRA SALMON RECIPE FEATURES A ZESTY RASPBERRY SAUCE THAT IS PERFECT TO ADORN OUR FRESH SALMON.

WE BEST BE CAREFUL BECAUSE ALL THE KODIAK BEARS LOVE TO EAT THE RASPBERRIES EVEN MORE THAN WE DO, AND THEY ARE SO CLEVER, THEY MAY CATCH US OFF GUARD. WE WON'T BE ABLE TO ENJOY OUR DELICIOUS DIN-NER IF WE BECOME THEIR DELICIOUS DINNER! CHALLENGE FORFEITED.

ONE-EYED WILLY AND TOUCAN SALLY WILL BRAVE IT OUT AND VENTURE INTO THE BRUSH TO FIND US THE BEST TASTING TANGIEST RASPBERRIES FOR THIS SPECIAL SAUCE. HEROIC.

WILD TUNDRA SALMON

WITH BEARY GOOD RASPBERRY SAUCE

SALMON INGREDIENTS

- 1 1/2 POUNDS SALMON FILLET
- 1 TEASPOON AND 1 TABLESPOON COOKING OIL
- 1 TEASPOON DRIED BASIL
- 1 TEASPOON CHOPPED FRESH PARSLEY
- 1/4 TEASPOON SALT
- 1/4 TEASPOON PEPPER
- 2 TTBLESPOONS BUTTER
- 1/2 CUP WHITE WINE
- 1 TABLESPOON CAPERS
- 1 LEMON, CUT IN HALF

DIRECTIONS

1. RUB THE SALMON WITH 1 TEASPOON COOKING OIL AND SPRINKLE WITH THE BASIL, PARSLEY, SALT, AND PEPPER.
2. IN A MEDIUM FRY PAN ON MEDIUM HIGH HEAT, ADD THE COOKING OIL AND BUTTER.
3. WHEN THE BUTTER HAS MELTED, PLACE THE SALMON FILETS INTO THE PAN, SKIN SIDE DOWN, AND COOK 6 TO 8 MINUTES.
4. REPEATEDLY SPOON THE OIL AND MELTED BUTTER IN THE PAN OVER THE SALMON WHILE COOKING.
5. ADD THE WHITE WINE AND CAPERS.
6. TURN THE SALMON OVER AND CONTINUE SPOONING THE BUTTERY OIL OVER THE SALMON AND COOK FOR 4 MINUTES.

BEFORE SERVING, SQUEEZE THE LEMON OVER THE SALMON.

BEARY GOOD RASPBERRY SAUCE

12 OUNCES FRESH RASPBERRIES
2 TABLESPOONS OF BUTTER
1 TABLESPOON MADEIRA WINE (NOT IN DIRECTIONS)
2 TEASPOONS OF HONEY
1 TEASPOON BALSAMIC VINEGAR (NOT IN DIRECTIONS)
1/4 TEASPOON SUGAR

DIRECTIONS

1. IN A SMALL SAUCEPAN AT MEDIUM HEAT, USE THE SPOON TO SMASH THE BERRIES WHILE STIRRING.
2. COOK 6 TO 10 MINUTES UNTIL IT TURNS TO LIQUID.
3. POUR THE SAUCE THROUGH A FINE MESH STRAINER OVER A SMALL BOWL.
4. PUT THE STRAINED SAUCE BACK INTO THE SAUCEPAN AND BRING TO A SIMMER.
5. ADD THE MADEIRA AND BALSAMIC VINEGAR.
6. ADD THE BUTTER, HONEY, AND SUGAR. STIR UNTIL THE BUTTER HAS MELTED. IT WILL THICKEN THE SAUCE AND WILL GIVE IT NICE SHINE.
7. POUR THE SAUCE OVER THE SALMON OR SERVE ON THE SIDE.

WILD TUNDRA SALMON WITH
BEARY GOOD RASPBERRY SAUCE

SHOWN WITH WILD RICE AND CORNY PEAS

DENNY ISLAND, BRITISH COLUMBIA

It is hard to leave Kodiak; however, we are pulling up anchor and setting sail for our last stop on this flavorsome journey, past the Yukon Territory down to Denny Island, British Columbia, a province of Canada.

Denny Island is part of the Great Bear Rainforest with lots of wildlife like bald eagles, wolves, black bears, and grizzlies. There is also the mysterious spirit bear—a rare white-colored black bear that lives in these parts and no other place on earth. It is good luck to see a spirit bear; and we come here to find one and cook his cousin—the bovine beast of beef, the red meaty sustenance for our final sensational spread. The beast shall be devoured with the smooth and silky red flag wine reduction sauce, a pirate's perfect pairing!

FILET MIGNON OF BEAST

WITH RED FLAG WINE REDUCTION SAUCE

RED FLAG WINE REDUCTION SAUCE INGREDIENTS

    2 TABLESPOONS OLIVE OIL
    3 CLOVES OF CRUSHED GARLIC
    1/4 CUP LARGELY CHOPPED YELLOW ONION
    1/4 CUP LARGELY CHOPPED GREEN BELL PEPPER
    1/4 CUP LARGELY CHOPPED GREEN BELL PEPPER
    3 CUPS OF A GOOD RED WINE
    3 TABLESPOON BUTTER
    2 TABLESPOONS OF BEEF BROTH
    1/4 TEASPOON SALT
    1/4 TEASPOON PEPPER
    1/4 TEASPOON OF SUGAR

RED FLAG WINE REDUCTION SAUCE DIRECTIONS

1. IN A MEDIUM-SIZE SAUCEPAN, BRING THE OLIVE OIL TO A SIZZLE ON MEDIUM HEAT.
2. ADD THE GARLIC AND ONION AND COOK UNTIL THE ONION IS TRANSLUCENT.
3. ADD THE BELL PEPPERS AND COOK 5 MINUTES.
4. ADD THE RED WINE AND BRING IT TO A ROLLING BOIL TO REDUCE BY HALF.
5. WHEN REDUCED, PUT THE SAUCE THROUGH A FINE MESH STRAINER OVER A BOWL.
6. DISCARD THE GARLIC, ONION, AND BELL PEPPERS.
7. PUT THE SAUCE BACK INTO THE SAUCEPAN AND REHEAT 5 MINUTES.
8. ADD THE BEEF BROTH AND SIMMER 10 MINUTES.
9. ADD SALT, PEPPER, AND SUGAR.
10. ADD THE TWO TABLESPOONS OF BUTTER AND MELT TO THICKEN THE SAUCE.
11. ADD A LITTLE CORNSTARCH MIXED IN WATER IF YOU WANT IT THICKER.
12. POUR THE SAUCE OVER THE FILETS OR SERVE IT ON THE SIDE AND ENJOY!

FILET MIGNON OF BEAST DIRECTIONS

2 EIGHT TO TEN-OUNCE BEEF FILETS

GRILL TO YOUR LIKING OVER AN OPEN FIRE, POT BELLY STOVE, BARBEQUE, OR WHATEVER YOU MIGHT HAVE ON YOUR SAILING VESSEL OR BASECAMP.

IF YOU ARE USING A BARBEQUE, YOU CAN COOK THE MEAT BY INDIRECT HEAT. YOU CAN ACHIEVE THIS METHOD BY ARRANGING THE COALS ON THE RIGHT AND LEFT SIDES INSIDE THE BARBEQUE. ONCE THE COALS ARE READY, PLACE THE FILETS IN THE MIDDLE OF THE BARBEQUE. GRILL TO YOUR PREFERENCE--RARE, MEDIUM RARE, MEDIUM WELL, AND WELL DONE. I DO NOT RECOMMEND COOKING UNTIL THE MEAT IS WELL DONE AS THE FLAVOR AND TEXTURE OF THE MEAT WILL BE COMPRO-MISED. REMEMBER, THE MEAT WILL CONTINUE TO COOK AFTER IT COMES OFF THE GRILL, SO TAKE THAT INTO CONSIDERATION AS YOU WILL WANT TO LET THE MEAT REST FOR FIVE MINUTES TO RETAIN THE JUICES.
AS THE BEAST OF BEEF IS COOKING YOU CAN MAKE THE RED FLAG WINE REDUCTION SAUCE.

FILET MIGNON OF BEAST WITH RED FLAG WINE REDUCTION SAUCE

SHOWN HERE WITH GREEN SALAD AND BAKED POTATO

Our adventurous gastro expedition has come to an end, and now it is time to make our way back to where we started from—our home port of Capitola, California.

We are more tickled than a parrot's feather on a dead man's chest to have had you aboard the *Ahoy McCoy* for this culinary journey around the world. We sincerely hope that you have enjoyed the trip as much as we have.

You are now fully equipped to create these tasty meals in your galley to satisfy your hungry crew. Feel free to modify the recipes to make them your own.

After so many salty days at sea, it sure feels good to be close to home. I miss my land lubbin' bed!

One more thing, we have a little secret, and now seems the right time to take off the barnacles and reveal the truth about One-Eyed Willy and Toucan Sally.

The fact of the matter is that I, your Captain Denny, am really One-Eyed Willy; and me first mate, Cherrie the Purple Pirate, is really Toucan Sally. Pirate surprise!

ABOUT THE AUTHORS

Cherrie and Denny McCoy have sailed the open seas of life together for forty years and counting. Longtime pirate lovers and fun-loving cooks, it only seemed natural to marry the two together.

When not at sea, they are busy living happily ever after in their home port of Capitola, California.

CPSIA information can be obtained
at www.ICGtesting.com
Printed in the USA
LVHW072303120721
692547LV00002B/17